Life expectancy begins to fall

Life expectancy begins to fall
Tom Sastry

Nine
Arches
Press

Life expectancy begns to fall
Tom Sastry

ISBN: 978-1-916760-12-7
eISBN: 978-1-916760-13-4

Copyright © Tom Sastry

Cover artwork: 'Half Full' © Tom Denbigh, 2025.
www.tomdenbigh.co.uk

All rights reserved. No part of this work may be reproduced, stored or transmitted in any form or by any means, graphic, electronic, recorded or mechanical, without the prior written permission of the publisher.

Tom Sastry has asserted his right under Section 77 of the Copyright, Designs and Patents Act 1988 to be identified as the author of this work.

First published March 2025 by:

Nine Arches Press
Studio 221, Zellig
Gibb Street, Deritend
Birmingham
B9 4AT
United Kingdom

www.ninearchespress.com

Printed on recycled paper in the United Kingdom by:
Imprint Digital

Nine Arches Press is supported using public funding by Arts Council England.

To Carly and our future, however it may be

Contents

Billionaire origin story	11
How to ignore an IPCC report	12
A pre-loved film from the vintage shop at History's End	14
The consumer as lonely king	18
Retail politics	19
Hatching	21
Your revolution	23
Solidarity	24
Nothing to do but play cards	26
Rooftops and moon	27
Hope buys an absurdly expensive woodland burial plot	29
Emergency response times	30
Therapeutic folk choir	32
Escape to the country	33
Staying alive	35
My friend, the conspiracy theorist	36
Bad diet	37
Life Expectancy Begins to Fall	
The last time we were here	38
Everyone knows about common sense	39
Risk assessment	40
Down by the riverside	41
Noah and his theories	42
Streaming	43
Fresh morning	44
The voice of a generation	45
Your one wild and precious lifestyle	47
The Galleries	49
Spiritual bypassing	51
Football practice	52
A short history of thought experiments	54
Firefly, lamp, campfire, city, star	56

Cinderella, ever after	57
Re-introducing the bears	59
My friend is still my enemy's friend	60
Emotional correctness	61
On my cousin's doorstep	63
Everyone loves the end of the world	64
Anthropocene Gothic	66
September	67
How to tell the apocalypse is happening when you get all your news from Instagram	68
The resistance	71
The park	73
Keep Britain Tidy	74
The consumer at prayer	75
Navigating the Peri-Apocalypse with Radical Self-Care	77
An increasing incidence of extreme weather events	78
Pipe & Slippers, New Year's Day, 4pm	79
The loss	81
The preserved body of a billionaire slowly defrosts in a devastated world	82
You can't take your spiritual clichés with you	83
Acknowledgements	86
Notes	88

Billionaire origin story

a boy in my school blew things up
he'd heard about the big bang   how dust from a great explosion
in a few short billion years
made stars   planets   lakes   dinosaurs
his own complicated thoughts

he'd heard the earth was dying   so he decided
to play god   creating new worlds
atomising other people's sports shoes
the food waste bin
finally   catastrophically   the rabbit hutch

they took him away   taught him
to be a thought leader
the dust he raised   his disruptive hope
clouded our century's air   dull dirt
hammered guesses of a monkey Shakespeare

the world we had   flaked into chaos
heat   flood   hunger
strange seasons of the troubled heart
more votes   for more dust
sunsets to die for

we tried everything
a funeral for the rabbit
calling storms   *weather*
imagining ourselves as dandelion seeds
history as a summer breeze

to walk forward in time again
wishing that Morrissey had stopped in 1987.

The possibility of other disasters
survives with me. Factories rust and fall.

Coal is burnt elsewhere.
Ice retreats, soil thins.

There are new plagues
and old hatreds.

In the chapel of a perfect night
I can hear the world sing

the song of its own ending
from the soundtrack to the movie of my life.

I give each danger a year or two
then tape over the warnings.

*In the country of what-you-don't-know-can't-hurt-you
our rivers are clear, our history true.*

*The air is safe and the climate right.
You still quote my brilliant sayings from last Saturday night.*

*A psychic says she can't abide
toilet cubicles, high windows, the shore at low tide.*

Solidarity

This is actually awkward.
The arseholes

who think you reveal
your true colours
by not quite agreeing with them

have got themselves arrested
for telling the truth

and now the hate has found them
there will be no escape

from the emergency logic
of their question
the one that steals your voice.

Which side are you on, boy?
Which side are you on?

Silence is violence. But is it better when I shout
Fuck! on the top deck while arguing in my head with
people who hate me? A period of silence from you would be

welcome, says the body language on the bus.
I agree. Is it too late to be agreeable? Hope says
nothing is final while we breathe, these are the good days.

Nothing to do but play cards

If it's too late to start cathedrals
or trust in a forty-year pension plan

too soon
to snatch the thing to hand
in the name of survival

if we're too honest
for self-sufficiency
or heroism

and our giddy hours don't come

if the deed
in our small reach
has no resounding name

let's call it with our silence
let's shuffle it again.

Rooftops and moon

at dusk everything is sufficient

when tasks refuse themselves

we sit on the swing seat as the sky rusts

bats tie elaborate knots to parcel up the day

slate cobwebs stretch against the murk

i don't immediately reach for your hand

it is good not wishing for anything

even when the galaxies are sparkles on a pool

and it's hard to tell

if the world is ordered as usual

or the sky moves against the clouds

I share the wisdom of my age.

*What we thought were different values
were just different circumstances.*

*What am I asking her to see?
When I retire, I'll write full-time.*

Her plan is dying in the climate wars.

Hope buys an absurdly expensive woodland burial plot

She is excited to be rendered
by fungi into tree-food. I feel a sharp
sadness when she says it. I check
it was not an urgent purchase
then ask questions. I learn
the particulars of the site and the price
smile at her *joyous cycle of life*
and secretly, inwardly
devour it with my scorn.
Life is a guzzling machine
forever eating itself.
Hope – your people need you.
Don't give up on us.

Emergency response times

i came off my bike
came off ha ha ha
smashed my left cheek
a great excuse for a half smile
afterwards
people told me their opinion
of anyone who walked past
strange because i never mentioned that
i remember the ones
who met on the pavement
gasping at the tableau
of them not knowing first aid and me
a road taken to the face
limbs arranged accidentally
death trap said one
i think he's breathing said another
i tried to say i understood
he doesn't know where he is
i was in the watch of my own people
just witnesses
[me with my mother]
resisting the urge to disappear
until eventually the sirens

*He says life feels flat but it will pass.
Does he mean life or its flatness? Neither
is enough. He needs a new miracle.*

*In the slowness of the boat we'll become
curious. Something grows to the side
of where we are. Something makes us smile.*

Therapeutic folk choir

The song is traditional. Each singer owns it.
Hurling the virgin snow
of their feeling. Claiming the discovery
of their ebbing moment. Today

it's yours. Sing it like glory, like praise
like the best joke in the world.
Find it in your chest and set it free.
Plaster the walls of hearing with its truth:

> *We are truly fucked to Hell*
> *We really are this time for sure*
> *Not one damn thing is going well*
> *We are truly fucked to Hell*

Stop pulling the wagon of hope. Run
with liberated force into what's left
briefly weightless, faster than doom.
Sing it! Sing it! Sing it!

Escape to the country

In the land of second homes, damp earth and sky are status goods / Chris makes fire, Amy splits tomorrow's logs / Smooth white cheeks redden / Health: the just reward for an outdoor life / *Can I do anything useful?* / I slide the foraged mushrooms into the pot / *There's always the risk of human error* says Marcus.

Hell is other people's values. I want them to be fools.

They have six acres / *We could live off this land if we had to* / There are coy smiles / There is something else / They have guns, actually / Our worlds divide / There's no self-build Arcadia for me if supply chains fail / I am club-fingered, my balance is poor / I can't afford land, I can't scare my fate.

I've never held a gun. I say. I don't know if I've seen one.

*A devotion America taught me
while I thought I was looking away.*

*My hand is now most comfortable
in a lethal position.*

*My arms lift the sight to my eye
and only my aim exists.*

Staying alive

Callum's friend thinks *the collapse*
will be a time for strong men
whose protection

people will do *anything* for. A woman
hops past the bar clutching a broken shoe.
We are doing a course

on household maintenance. They love
how useless I am. When I say
you make it sound like a racket

they laugh like I've gone through a pipe.
It's my round but he's asking: *same again?*
The racket is their happy place.

My friend, the conspiracy theorist

It's easy to love my neighbour when I notice
I'm lonely. There's one name I know here
so once I've looked both ways across the bar
I smile. Soon, we're pulling down the towns
we were glad to leave, slandering people
who find us both too difficult. This is not

forgiveness or compromise. In his wild talk
of civil war I know my side – but tonight
suspend my allegiance to become a person
who walks into a pub and is part of its life.
My city knows me now, glitters its approval
from high-stacked windows full of money.

Bad diet

In planning an old age
with enough money for groceries at current prices
in case the apocalypse is late

while encouraging my body
my only home in the universe
to race the holocene into oblivion

I am glueing myself to the present
where water is drinkable and no bombs fall
blocking the artery of time.

Motion, frustrated, erupts in rage.
A clock screams in my face. My comrades
sing defiant hope over the alarms

but I am not here to overcome.
What, in the end, do I want?
The sky at dusk. Forever.

Life Expectancy Begins to Fall

The last time we were here

I was eight. Miss Cox lived next door.
She didn't fit my seed of a world

with its parents, grandparents and no great-
anything. Nothing in her house

had a use I knew: old metal, coal and lace
tired fabrics, damp to touch.

What made me scared to look her in the face
was an undead number.

Eighty.
The same span I would come to expect

before the fall, at the peak of expectation
with its immense, simulated view.

Everyone knows about common sense

Historians say
there is much to learn from unreliable accounts.

On the front page, a familiar shock.
Murder, the one death deemed unnatural

demands for new law. Inside:
Hospitals In Crisis; Millions Choose Not To Work.

In the notices, those withholding words.
Sudden. Difficult.

Faces, names, dates.
The cycle speeding up.

Online, in the comments
trouble grows from trouble.

Risk assessment

I adored tobacco. If a tyrant said
You must smoke again I wouldn't mind.

It costs ten years. It gave me calm
when I wanted it. When things get bad

be careful. If they get worse
just be. Four doors down

there's a pub with unfiltered air
and a welcome. I've not opened arms

in a long time. It was always a short walk
through the cordon or into the fallout.

I'm coming, my friends, I'm coming
to gulp the viral cloud.

Down by the riverside

Annuities offer exceptional value
but who can make you sing of joy

in the presence of death?
The church revives as life-coaches fail.

We surrender our plans
our stories.

Our journeys are not chosen.
We are consignments

trusted to the next country's river.
We need a God whose love

survives our curses, a promise
unfathomable as sky.

Noah and his theories

If you have children, says Noah
who has no-one, *make one*

a hypochondriac. The rest
can be daring. *It spreads your risks.*

We were not constructed as ruins.
Our city is still tall; still, in places

gleaming. *Give the future the truth
Mr. Writer. Our present need is hope.*

Noah will live to nine hundred
he says. Noah is scavenging rope.

Noah asks for wood and nails.
He is building a boat, using sheets for the sails.

Streaming

Too tired to talk, we watch a film.
Tonight, it's 1914.

History – the flow of events we carry –
will soon carry us off.

We are aerosol thoughts, breath
suspended, our pity unlocked

by a safe distance from the ground.
It's the magic of perspective.

There's a dot, way down there. Inside it
empires set fire to themselves.

You squeeze my hand.
I turn for the emotion on your face.

Fresh morning

Cold air wants to kill me but I have clothes.
Leaves crack under my shoe like unregarded fossils.
The park swanks in the rhinestones of heaven
because the sun has put its work
into appearances. That's one twist on hope:
the chance of good lighting, good teeth.
Twist again and ask to be understood.
I don't pretend happiness is a choice
so when joy finds me, what I find in that is fortune.
I am a day like any other. A sequence of hours.
I am the bird that hops on the frost, then sings.

The voice of a generation

it turned out the best poet
the one we wanted to be like
was an actor
reciting the output of an AI

we each thought we were the only one
laughing at the absurdity
but the algorithm said
being the only one is a kind of meaning
we just wanted to be something

the poems were still very good
we tried to prove the opposite
chanting them derisively at each other
but as fast we explained away their merits
we found something new in them

we could still have been wrong
think of the people friends have fallen in love with

are you avid to be yourself
in an exciting new way?
when a surface reflects your heart
do you feel human again?

*You know persistence better than hope
tongue-biting, budgeting, able to cope*

and then the executives gamble and run.

*You feel like a failure as fortune turns
the country goes under, the planet burns*

your ethic still works you until you are done.

Your one wild and precious lifestyle

I'm not like you, says the office to the office.
You *are* this place. I'm not *this place.*

The office, which never wanted to be the office either
but has no plan to stop being the office

fills with sadness, wants it to show. The first rule
of the office is *no-one is really the office* –

we are all hoarding some part of ourselves.
The office, who has just handed in her notice

is full of the fucks she doesn't give.
She lists the glorious things she will do

when she flies off, into her own sky
at a thousand joyful miles an hour. Some involve yoga

and sound boring, which makes the office
feel slightly better. But after the office has left

early, because *what can they do – fire me?*
the office gasps under the weight of small effort

over-watering the ugly plant, starting a collection
for the office's leaving gift. The rest of the office

which occasionally comforts its particular friends
in the airless meeting rooms

and otherwise blocks out human emotion
looks up, then launches conversations

like capsules from an airlock;
or reads about drought and avian flu;

or thinks of the home where it is loved
or not; or looks at expensive holidays.

The kind you want to tell the office about.
The kind you look forward to all year.

The Galleries

the guy at the next urinal
says when you wank
do you fuck or make love
he has good communication skills
asking questions not talking about himself
if he was my cellmate
i would have to answer him
for years in a tiny space
him knowing my personal sounds
there goes my mind
wandering again
beyond all bureaucratic grace
in the curated abandonments of the world
the prison
the annihilated city
bedridden but fit-for-work
while my body escapes
from camera to camera
to privacy
the heroic illusion
allowing me to share this story
as if i belonged to myself

*Last night, I walked alone
under the trees in the park
chasing short drops of moonlight.*

*I was not murdered. I have been
not murdered many times. Life
in doubt, remains probable. I make plans.*

Spiritual bypassing

the self is a mirage
wrote the very online person
with an expensive traveling yoga habit
for whom the universe often manifests
expensive gifts

with a jolt I remembered my father
saying *I have come to the conclusion
that I do not exist*
and how the illusion of me
preferred to connect with the illusion of him

by switching on the cricket
and keeping an unexamined silence

our lantern brains turning action into statistics
his breath continuing its duty

Football practice

My father, who has no idea, is coaching
and I, clueless as he, am falling over my feet.

The other boys, to whom I am a puzzle
are giving me looks I cannot solve

and afterwards, we have nothing to say.
This is no wonder because everywhere

prophets who don't know what is happening
activists who cannot act

friends who fail, clumsy lovers
are stumbling past trees whose roots

press helplessly through the soil, insects
clutching the wrong scraps of leaf

and dogs pretending
to be their idea of your idea of happy.

Forgive yourself. Spare the effort
of those who can't forgive you.

*In a country of happy murderers
who kill you or forgive you
but hold no grudge*

*I could be on good terms
with everyone (although
possibly dead).*

A short history of thought experiments

You hold Baby Hitler in your arms
warm as a loaf with untroubled eyes.
The time machine leaves in twenty minutes.

The philosophy boy is annoyed with you
saying how it feels – the shudder of the act.
He gives you a trolley problem. His sketch

is crude. The people look like sausages.
Does that make it easier? You watch him.
You think, he tied them to the rails.

Come on he says. *It's not real.* Drone pilots
work from home, playing something
which pretends to be a game, while bots

exploit your feeling parts by devilling
your neighbour. *It blows your mind* he says.
His mind stays on its track. Now you're annoyed

so you take the toothbrush that ploughed your gums
scour the cities of mould from the grout.
You try to leave no survivors.

*I want a church but no god. Sometimes
god but no church. I want doubt respected.
I think faith ignoring facts is wicked*

*until I need it. Paul lets me talk.
He deals in moments, thinks everyone knows
good days answer their own questions.*

Firefly, lamp, campfire, city, star

Hope is a funnel. It begins with something grand you want for yourself.
You are Cinderella or a billionaire. One day you will live in the square
whose windows you peered into as a child. Then you want
something ordinary but huge like five different kinds
of love under one roof. Then small moments
recurring and then small moments
one more time; and then
just more time,
for them if
not for
you

or
is
it
an

egg
-timer?
All your life
your eye adored
the exception to the rule
so now the rule is darkness you see
what firefly, lamp, campfire, city, star, reveal
about the majesty of lonely light. Find something in
the distance, it proves there's something within. It scares you.
Friends want you angrier about injustice. You see yourself in their eyes
serene, comfortable, apolitical. They are fear and love. It is spectacular.

Cinderella, ever after

The boy she likes is a stablehand.
Sun on his skin, work in his arms.
The only thing she'd take is a fast horse.

This boy is her threat. This boy is her vest
of explosives. He puts the family
on the front pages. She takes this thought

out on the gallops, lets them sweat.
The boy doesn't work nights at the palace
does shifts in a garage. By chance

she pulls up, on her latest horse
for a bushel of a Premium 98, a vape
and a tube of Pringles. Most people say

she's a refreshing change. Her boy
is a pumpkin. He's worth less than a horse.
He is not thought to feel pain or pleasure

except as physical. This explains
the way they punish him. Cinderella
knows how her bed is made.

She steps back onto the surface
of her life. Her face is painted
into history. She tries not to have

too many children, forbids
her daughter, dotes on her son.
Her father, the chief engineer

appears in her biography as a handyman
so she can be a fairytale. On the guillotine
she will regret nothing, least of all the boy.

A sheep's skull seen on a walk
makes us feel alive

there is something in this moment we want to keep
a smudge of the divine in our pity

we savour our burden of understanding
debate whether to take photos

Re-introducing the bears

At first, they are interloping shadows
caught on camera traps, snouting the night:
a feelgood story for a slow news day.
Soon, their presence is felt. Out there

on the wrong side of history, a group called
Human Lives holds a press conference. Its head
(a land banker's lawyer) says it's clear
someone will die: a human sacrifice

to the do-gooders' need to make a difference.
He wants the forest for real estate, trees
for floorboards, bears for coats. Goldilocks
his star turn, lifts her greying head

takes the mic, says *no child should cry as I did*.
She wants our beautiful nightmares stopped
shadows and magic razed. She wants everything
just common sense. Darkness kept to its place –

light at the touch of a switch. Homes full
of clear lines. Birds allowed their small song.
Landscaped acres, lawns fit for bare feet.
A gun in its case. A nature trail.

Yesterday, a friend mentioned an old name.
He was drunk. Then he remembered, stopped
said he still held a high regard. I'd felt tearful

and tired, which was OK. The sun would rise
but I could sleep late, then take myself off somewhere.
I could choose not to keep fighting in my head…

My friend is still my enemy's friend

…Today was that day off. Some days you're hungry
and some days you're full. I wasn't full, just flat.
I tied my running shoes but I knew I was spent.

I didn't have the heart. I didn't have a yes
I didn't even have a no, so I set out
knowing it would get hard and I'd quit, which I did.

Yesterday, a friend mentioned an old name.
He was drunk. Then he remembered, stopped
said he still held a high regard. I'd felt tearful

and tired, which was OK. The sun would rise
but I could sleep late, then take myself off somewhere.
I could choose not to keep fighting in my head…

My friend is still my enemy's friend

…Today was that day off. Some days you're hungry
and some days you're full. I wasn't full, just flat.
I tied my running shoes but I knew I was spent.

I didn't have the heart. I didn't have a yes
I didn't even have a no, so I set out
knowing it would get hard and I'd quit, which I did.

Emotional correctness

do you remember that summer on the moon · it's ok i know you don't · but stay with me · please · all my life i have heard · how hard times do not exist without moments of joy · and it is wretched to speak · only of the darkness · and in the worst of places · there are bright rooms full of talents · but high days come quicker · than high feelings · my most persistent human moment is the one · that witnesses its own absence · when fear is a visceral lake · sloshing at my brim · i could ask more plainly · how you miss yourself · but everyone has their urgent reasons · for forgetting · what if memory was an animal · an honesty made of instinct not fact · it could promise me · that i left the better part of myself · on the moon where it is always summer · even rock has a softness if you remember how to touch · and on the moon i do

The animal in me feels Winter coming.
I carry her protesting out the front door
for the trouble of it, the weight of the task

and return, with a fat loaf, to the light I left
thrilling to the knowledge of shelter
my flossed hair filled with pearls.

On my cousin's doorstep

She has a bell-pull, with feathers
and a brass plate with her name
which is Hope. I rang it and stood there
while in the other flat
a man cried with his whole body.

I had these thoughts:

1) an adult's grief
    is the frequent state of a child
2a) thought is our plea to feeling
    to let us live
2b) the mind's work is about survival
    not cold reason as moonstruck
    cynics say.

By now I'd walked
my senses home. I will make an idea
that can hold them. I will find something
that feeds from my hand.
I will give my moments wings.

Everyone loves the end of the world

We all hope to enjoy the apocalypse
from a distance. A good storm
spares the roof but rattles the glass.
Children know: destruction is funny, sometimes beautiful.

A distant inferno would enchant your night
if you saw it from the next coast.
So much torment is shut away, you might even be comforted
by a Hell with space for your friends.

We build great telescopes to watch stars die
send divers to explore drowned cities, give prizes
for pictures of flaming sinkholes
or bones bleaching by a dry lake.

An old man reads of a decade he won't see
lethal heat, scarcity of food.
It aches softly, like a sunset.
A new desert at the edge of town, some murders on the news.

If the world is broken, let it be final.
A vengeful or careless god
snapping continents like biscuits.

What I fear is a Next Day.
The sweeping up and the reckoning.
The sobriety. The resumption.

Anthropocene Gothic

Halfway up the Anthropocene, it's still green. The air is pure –
a word whose futility you have not yet learnt. The future
is a steepling ring of teeth. This is the beauty you came for.

At the first peak, there is news. You hear it from friends:
a million strangers are dead. It never stops. You tell them
you think you may be climbing forever in search of an end.

Smiles drop from their faces. Faces drop from their bones.
Their sinews fray and drag in the wind. *Stop climbing!* they say
You're the reason! It's too much. You march up the last unknowns

seeking the quiet at the top of the world. You need time to
observe your thoughts, step outside your thoughts, move through
your eternal present. As if time belonged to you.

September

Civilisation is doomed, thank you for cutting my hair. It's September in Bristol, cool, bright and colourful. Everything still works with just a bit of money. If I'd made fruit gin ten years ago, I would pop the stopper, sink us in sweet poison, we could be a sunset together. Hope was careless, pessimism is complicated by love. I now accept conversations with strangers. It is no longer a surprise when I wake in pain. Let's dig the first grave together, spare the one who is left. Let's stuff ourselves with memories. Who knows how many we will need?

How to tell the apocalypse is happening when you get all your news from Instagram

1.

Hope is the new chastity: the moralist's favourite virtue.

People who notice the apocalypse are pessimists, pessimists are cynics, cynics are fashionable.

Autumn is more red than brown. Its suns are golden. The world, whatever that means, is mad for joy.

All you have are the refuges of sadness.

This is my joy you say sitting alone in the shade of a charismatic tree.

This is my joy drinking a coffee with too many flavours.

This is my joy as you prepare to watch a blockbuster sneered at by unpopular young men whose phantom power everyone loves to defy.

2.

The people who shamed you as a fashionable cynic are recovering from toxic joy culture.

Their tears are brave. They have no grass to touch. Their winter is a scroll of confected whiteness, a landscape of imaginary snow.

Their sudden poems want to be immortal and cannot be edited.

You are three months behind the apocalypse, still pretending not to notice.

This is my joy you say as you film yourself eating a cockroach burger in a pop-up, in a burnt out penthouse near the central business district of the emptying city.

You have never felt so disliked.

By the places the Gods live
the sea, the mountain, the sky

in the city rousing to its darkness

a part of you offers itself
to the violence of the world

another part resists

The resistance

We are spaced out under the awning in Hannah's garden

I love the shock of the rain

it feels like despair exhausting itself.

We're outdoors for my sake. I'm the oldest

the only one who talks about living longer than I can work.

The sky clears. There's a bowl warming my hand.

I am taking my sense of smell for granted again.

The extravagant script of the peas climbs the bamboo poles in the long evening light. I want to be alive, as if I'm not already.

There are sixty harvests left.

Hannah is using the soil while we have it.

Hope calls it *the most radical act*. This makes sense

as admiration and love.

Nothing happens, in the most lavish way.

*There are days I want to reach for everyone
cliché them a piece of my heart; cherish
forgive, hold their eyes, change their luck.*

*Trouble makes us fear the details. We prefer
to play the magician than be a friend.
Enough wisdom already. How are things?*

The park

summer i stopped raging
accepted i was not likeable
sat on twenty-two benches
all unique
weather went and came
a jealous love of my own time
the bins told me stories
the slow runners
i wished them well

what to make
of those parts of ourselves no-one wants
that feel like gifts in the giving
that keep suggesting themselves
paul said i might talk less
never once thanked me for my silence
yes i would have been wounded again

shutting yourself up is a temporary fix
when the leaves fell i took my silence indoors
my housemates pushed their laughter into it
i had twenty-two benches
weather came and went
deep in one coat sitting on another
the runners fewer and faster
when time was all i had

Keep Britain Tidy

Leave the house, it's the inside of your head on the outside.
A guy screams into a bin but the bin is full.

His thoughts plumb the belly of the trash
and their wrappers ascend like soft printed birds

on the hissing wind. This weather we call *spiteful*
is the earth's disappointed love. That's what I tell myself

as I stuff my fist with the litter of his spirit
feeling briefly like a saint, then for a longer time

cold and foolish. Everyone's knackered.
It's the rain, the four-week cold, the hundred-day cough; the revelation

that God's another window where you offer up your trouble
and wait, and leave with no help

just a leaflet full of questions that put it all back on you
like the one I find here in a ball in my hand

with heathen T-Rex watching meteors fall
on the wrong side of a golden cloud.

The consumer at prayer

I am here to love the world.
I haven't done it for weeks.
I have no excuses.
I start here
hopeless, in the fresh produce aisle.

I am here to love the world
but when I lose it at the frozen food
and you, a stranger, are kind
I respond like a stranger
to kindness. Am I part of the same rage

as men with guns speaking for God?
I used to find more in my silence.
There's a feeling I need
but don't have.
I don't know who this honesty is for.

On Friday the PM spoke at last.
You are no longer an emergency he said
told us we were not afraid.

On Monday the signs appeared
Emergencies Only
above every official door.

Navigating the Peri-Apocalypse with Radical Self-Care

1.

Don't waste your minutes outside
trying to notice everything.
A different light falls on your hair.
The air is whispering.

2.

Find something that seems to answer you
but never shuts you up.
An animal is best. A picture will do.
This is your God, needy when you are.

3.

Also, a mug of tea is Holy.
Also, your bed adores you.
The sky is waiting and creatures fly in it.
If you woke from this dream, you would want to go back.

4.

Do not ration yourself to small words, proportionate feelings.
You can't afford modesty.
A movement at the window means the day can reach you.
It knows who you are, it's heard good things.

5.

A new day. Deep breath.
Hello World. Good to see you.
One day at a time.
Possibly, maybe, perhaps.

An increasing incidence of extreme weather events

We watched the charts all week
as the old hurricane's great lash
curled back across the ocean, not weakening
until we saw Bristol in its path.

The police told us to leave
for the nowhere we had to go
in the nothing we had to get there.
They would take the gloves off for looters.

Abandoned people are always crazy
like a fool who squares up to a storm.
Crazy like us, on the roofs of Easton
waving at the news helicopter

as the studio repeats the warnings
we were apparently ignoring
when we walked onto the M32
in a world already shaking and tearing

for a woman desperate to pass her child
into the mystery of a stranger's car
which was crammed to the corners
with the old necessities of home.

Pipe & Slippers, New Year's Day, 4pm

Shipwrecked in their festival gear
trails of paint on each cheek
they cling to the raft of the vanished year
whose riddance they came out to cheer.
May beds be waiting, somewhere near.
May they live well enough, week by week.

May ordinary hope never fill us with fear.
May each of us like what we seek.

*Do you remember when we said it was brave
to talk about healing? As if the problem
was other people choosing to remain broken*

*and not us waiting to feel firm ground
under our feet. We thought our decades
meant nothing if we couldn't stop falling.*

The loss

One day, the human world
smashed, you meet

a former frequent flyer
who says he cannot feel

regret. Fetched up here
in his consequences

he needs to remember
how it was marvellous.

And you
all fight and hope gone

look at the moment he shows you
which was your moment too.

You say *yes*
it was. We all were.

The preserved body of a billionaire slowly defrosts in a devastated world

His generators have better uses.
The great cables are hacked through. In the vault

a damp ego wakes to his several blinks
of deferred life. He thought we'd greet him

with life-supporting devices, harvest
his sperm to improve the species. Instead

five members of a semi-ironic fandom
gather to witness the last miracle

of a collapsed age. This is no country
for thawed-out men with medical histories stored

on long-corrupted hard drives.
It's not his time. It's the one he made.

You can't take your spiritual clichés with you

At the End of the World, I meet a guru.
I'm crapping myself. He calls this *unwise*.
How should I face a day with no future?
He says *like a mayfly*. He's just a man
blowing air into the shape of an answer.
I know that trick. Perhaps I can do this.

The guru is the last thing I need
the not-so-secret wisdom of my
evasive heart. He's my permission
to make myself an eye which holds no grief
and so, at the End of the World, he's there
telling me to *notice, notice, notice.*

There's nothing left to notice except
It's over. I'm free. I loved it so much.

Acknowledgements

Many fine poets were unwittingly complicit in this undertaking. Some offered sensitive feedback despite feeling out of sympathy with it. The generosity of this, in particuar, awes me. Others, I think, sort of enjoyed it. I will not identify either group within this list of wonderful folk. Suzannah Evans, Ian Irwin, Hannah Linden, Stefan Mohamed, Danny Pandolfi, Caleb Parkin, Mark Anthony Pearce, Jacqueline Saphra, Tom Weir.

Climate activists and denialists seem to agree on one thing: their contempt for doomers. I take this personally because I am often a doomer in my quiet moments. So I decided to commission a cover which fully embraces the idea that we are doomed. When I saw the first sketch of Tom Denbigh's brilliant *Half-full* I knew this was the right choice. Tom – thank you.

Tom's model was a contemporary woodcut of the 1607 Bristol Channel flood from the snappily entitled pamphlet *A true report of certaine wonderfull ouerflowings of Waters, now lately in Summersetshire, Norfolke and other places in England: destroying many thousands of men, women and children, overthrowing and bearing downe whole townes and villages, and drowning infinite numbers of sheepe and other Cattle.* This is the original:

Thanks are also due to those – too many to name – who have become part of this book through their conversation, understanding, friendship and patience, to the publications in which some of these poems have appeared, to Marius Grose for the author photo and poetry film, and to Jane Commane whose genius is not just that she makes the right suggestions but that she never makes unhelpful ones. I have no idea how she does it.

Notes

'Billionaire origin story' includes a reference to the Infinite Monkey Theorem – the idea that a monkey hitting keys on a typewriter for an infinite anount of time will eventually produce *The Complete Works of Shakespeare* (and any other text).

'How to ignore an IPCC report': the title is a reference to the Intergovernmental Panel on Climate Change.

'A pre-loved film from the vintage shop at History's End' is after Suzannah Evans. The poem to which I am particularly indebted is 'De-extinction' from her first collection *Near Future*.

Page 13: (untitled poem): The opening phrase "Good people are doing nothing again" is a reference to the reputed saying of Edmund Burke "The only thing necessary for the triumph of evil is for good men to do nothing".

'Solidarity': the final couplet quotes from 'Which side are you on?' by Florence Reece which I know from the version by Billy Bragg.

'Emergency response times': I don't normally state whether and how a poem is autobiographical but this is a special case. The speaker's implied relationship with their mother does not resemble my own.

'Life expectancy begins to fall': This poem has a very specific scenario. Life expectancy has fallen to a level last seen in the early 1980s (a drop of eight or nine years). This is not the apocalypse – it is the reversal of a few decades of progress in human health. It was written in response to the decision of governments to disregard non-acute illness in developing their approach to the Covid-19 pandemic.

Marius Grose has made a wonderful film of this poem which can be viewed on the Nine Arches Press Youtube channel.

'Your one wild and precious lifestyle' is, of course, a riff on the famous phrase by Mary Oliver from the poem 'The summer day' which I have read and enjoyed. It is also the title of a self-help book which I have not read and would not expect to enjoy.

'The Galleries' refers to a 1980s shopping centre in Bristol. According to the *Bristol Post*, it is slated for demolition but is likely to remain open "well into 2025". It contains a branch of Waterstones whose poetry section is within a few metres of the setting of this poem.

'A short history of thought experiments' contains a reference to the trolley problem: a thought experiment in which an onlooker has the opportunity to save several people who are tied to a track by diverting a runaway trolley onto another track where it will kill a single person.

'Anthropocene Gothic': I thought I was the originator of the phrase Anthropocene Gothic for a happy moment between writing the poem and googling its title. So far as I can tell, credit belongs to the authors of the book *Dark scenes from damaged earth: The Gothic Anthropocene* (ed. Edwards, Graulund and Höglund, University of Minnesota Press, 2022).

'Keep Britain Tidy': A version of this poem appeared in *Poetry Review* under the title 'As the end of the world becomes conventional wisdom, an ordinary man learns how it feels to be a prophet'. The shorter title – and less abrupt ending – in this book are both a consequence of my desire to maintain the flow from poem to poem. I like the earlier version too.

'Navigating the apocalypse with radical self-care' contains a blatant example of auto-plagiarism. The last line of this poem is also the last line of the poem 'Jeremy Paxman interviews the wild woman who lives in the woods' from my first collection *A man's house catches fire*.

'Pipe & Slippers, New Years Day, 4pm': The Pipe & Slippers is a pub on Cheltenham Road in Bristol. It is a place where a remnant of the revellers from a big party night in the city can sometimes be found well into the following day.